A Country Rebel

A Play

Jeffrey Grenfell-Hill

A SAMUEL FRENCH ACTING EDITION

FOUNDED 1830

SAMUELFRENCH-LONDON.CO.UK
SAMUELFRENCH.COM

Copyright © 1990 by Jeffrey Grenfell-Hill
All Rights Reserved

A *COUNTRY REBEL* is fully protected under the copyright laws of the British Commonwealth, including Canada, the United States of America, and all other countries of the Copyright Union. All rights, including professional and amateur stage productions, recitation, lecturing, public reading, motion picture, radio broadcasting, television and the rights of translation into foreign languages are strictly reserved.

ISBN 978-0-573-13222-3

www.samuelfrench-london.co.uk

www.samuelfrench.com

FOR AMATEUR PRODUCTION ENQUIRIES

UNITED KINGDOM AND WORLD EXCLUDING NORTH AMERICA

plays@SamuelFrench-London.co.uk

020 7255 4302/01

Each title is subject to availability from Samuel French, depending upon country of performance.

CAUTION: Professional and amateur producers are hereby warned that *A COUNTRY REBEL* is subject to a licensing fee. Publication of this play does not imply availability for performance. Both amateurs and professionals considering a production are strongly advised to apply to the appropriate agent before starting rehearsals, advertising, or booking a theatre. A licensing fee must be paid whether the title is presented for charity or gain and whether or not admission is charged.

The professional rights in this play are controlled by Samuel French Ltd, 52 Fitzroy Street, London, W1T 5JR.

No one shall make any changes in this title for the purpose of production. No part of this book may be reproduced, stored in a retrieval system, or transmitted in any form, by any means, now known or yet to be invented, including mechanical, electronic, photocopying, recording, videotaping, or otherwise, without the prior written permission of the publisher. No one shall upload this title, or part of this title, to any social media websites.

The right of Jeffrey Grenfell-Hill to be identified as author of this work has been asserted by him in accordance with Section 77 of the Copyright, Designs and Patents Act 1988

CHARACTERS

Sarah Dawkins, a countrywoman
Gran Twigden, her mother
Mrs Barker, an old friend from the village
Hilda Dawkins, a housemaid
Lady Corbishley, Lady of the Manor
Mrs Miles-Foster, one of the Workhouse Guardians

The action of the play takes place in a simple cottage room somewhere in the Edwardian English countryside

Time—past

Period: Edwardian

The lights fade during the action to denote the passage of time

AUTHOR'S NOTE

If the producer thinks it necessary the following introduction may be used as a prologue to the play.

Narrator We are going to see an England totally unlike the present day. Edward VII is on the throne, the summers are always burning hot and in the countryside the gentry "lord it" over the poor labourers. When a poor widow can no longer support herself she has to seek admission to the dreaded workhouse, an institution set up to receive all those who have no means of support. There is no dole money for the poor, nor pensions for the old folk. The Welfare State is still far into the future.

This is the story of a poor country widow who fights the system and triumphs. It is the story of a rebel who is not going to be brow-beaten, nor defeated by her "so called" betters. In 1908 the government will pass the Old Age Pensions Act which will allow all those over seventy to claim their five shillings a week. But our story is set in the years before this. It is a country tale, based on fact, not fiction.

A COUNTRY REBEL

A simple cottage room somewhere in the Edwardian English countryside before the Old Age Pensions Act was passed in 1908

There is a fender placed C to denote the hearth, around this supposed fireplace are a wooden table, chairs and on the back wall a ramshackle dresser with oddments of china. The room possesses nothing of any quality; indeed, there must be an appearance of poverty. There is a front door upstage

Sarah, a woman past her fortieth year, is sitting in one of the chairs before the fire slowly peeling potatoes into a bowl she has on her lap. Suddenly the cottage door opens, and her mother, Gran Twigden, comes in puffing and panting; she is an old woman around the age of seventy, but sprightly and full of life

Gran (*carrying a great bundle of sticks*) Oh! Sarah, I'm fair puffed out, what with that wind blowin' and 'er Ladyship goin' at me hammer an' tongs!

Sarah Now Mother, don't tell me you've been in the manor woods again. Why do you do it? You knows 'er Ladyship don't allow it.

Gran (*laughing uproariously*) I does it 'cos I'm a wicked ol' girl. But I gets us firewood, don't I? (*She pulls forward a great pile of sticks, throwing them before the fire*) That lot will keep us warm for a day or two. (*She sits opposite her daughter and pulls off the shawl she has covering her head*) Oh! What an actress I would 'ave made, if only me father 'adn't been 'is Lordship's gardener. I could 'ave been actressin' all over the world now if I 'adn't been born a poor girl.

Sarah Mother, what 'ave you been up to. (*She frowns*) You've not been upsettin' 'er Ladyship again, 'ave you? You'll 'ave us evicted. Why you can't go stickin' along the highway.

Gran Ah! There ain't no wood along the highway. No, it's best to get into the park down by the brook. I squeeze in see, through the fence by the ol' mill. As long as I keeps my 'ead low no soul can see me from the manor.

Sarah That may be, but 'er Ladyship 'as given out strict instructions that us must not go into the park. (*She leans forward*) Why do you think they've got that fence up?

Gran So as a wicked ol' girl like me can squeeze through, 'cos I ain't up to jumpin' over no more, that's a fact. (*She stoops down and starts to lay out the sticks before the fire*) There! That'll warm 'em, dry 'em out. They'll be ready for burnin' by the mornin'.

Sarah (*getting up with the potatoes finished in the bowl*) Now don't you go in the park no more, you find us wood elsewhere. (*She starts to put them into a saucepan on the table*)

Gran Oh! Girl, I loves the excitement of it; it's the Devil gets in me as I was goin' past the brook that little 'ole in the park fence just seemed to be for me. After that great wind last night I knew there'd be a great deal of wood come down from those trees. Before I knew it I 'ad a great bundle, and before I could 'ear 'er comin' 'er Ladyship was there behind me. I jumped out of my skin when I 'eard her say, "Gran Twigden, put that wood down. It is not yours to take!"

Sarah (*fetching water in a pail to pour into the saucepan*) But you come back with a great bundle, Mother.

Gran (*laughing uproariously*) I knows that. As soon as one bundle was all tied up I tossed it over the fence. 'Er Ladyship couldn't see the first bundle, only the one I was carryin'. So I only lost half my wood.

Sarah If you ask me, she'll be gettin' at our Hilda. Don't you ever consider what it might be like for your grand-daughter? She's up at the manor as a housemaid an' her gran is caught red 'anded stealing wood from out the park. 'Er Ladyship will 'ave a go at 'er.

Gran (*getting up*) Oh! Don't worry about Hilda. She's like me. She can take care of herself. (*She suddenly grimaces*) Oh! That was a nasty twinge. (*Putting her hand up to her cheek*) The worse thing about gettin' old is gettin' toothache. Oh! Sarah, where's that oil of cloves you got me?

Sarah (*going to dresser*) It's in the drawer, 'ere where you put it last. Got it. Here, put some on quickly. Do you know the one that's hurtin'?

A Country Rebel

Gran Oh! Glory be, sometimes they *all* 'urt. (*She takes the bottle and puts some oil on a rag she has in her pocket*) This stuff ain't much use when it gets real bad. (*She goes back to the fire, tries to put some on her tooth, but is still in pain*)

Sarah Teeth! What problems they are. They hurt you when they're comin' in, an' they hurts you when they're fallin' out.

Gran I wouldn't mind if they *fell* out, it's the *pulling* of them out I can't abide. Oh! There it goes again. (*She turns*) 'Aven't you got no sympathy, Sarah?

Sarah 'Course I got sympathy. But what you expect at your age? I'll bind your face up with that red flannel if I can find it. (*She rummages about in the dresser*) It worked last time. It warmed your jaw. Ah! Here it is. (*She finds a roll of red flannel, rolled up like a bandage*) We'll put this around your 'ead an' you'll soon feel better. (*She takes a safety-pin from a bowl*) Red flannel always does the trick. I swears by it.

Gran Well *I'll* be swearin' in a minute if this pain don't go away. It's playin' up like bally-hoo, that's what it is. Ow!

Sarah starts to put the red flannel around her head; it goes under the chin a few times and is finally fastened with a safety-pin on top of the head

Sarah The red will draw out the pain, make it go away. You've got that oil of cloves workin' on the inside, an' this 'ere red flannel drawin' out the pain on the outside.

Gran Well, I 'opes it does the trick. When I 'ad earache last winter, you wanted to pour the contents of the chamber pot down me ear-hole. You get some funny ideas in your 'ead sometimes . . .

Sarah Oh! Mother, they calls it the warm urine treatment. Mrs Dodds got told it at the Mother's Union, an' very pleased I was she passed it on to me. It would 'ave done the trick if only you'd 'ave let me do it.

Gran What, put me water down me ear! It ain't right. (*She winces*)

Sarah Well, you'll have to look after yourself, Mother. (*She goes to a hook on the wall and gets a shawl*) It's rainin' now, but the pail's nearly empty. I'm goin' to pump for water. You just sit there an' keep warm by the fire.

Gran Ay! You're right. I'll try to doze off.

Sarah leaves the cottage carrying the empty pail

Gran winces a little, then settles down to get some sleep in front of the fire. As she dozes off the door opens

  Mrs Barker enters. She is a countrywoman of the poorer sort, with a piece of sacking covering her head

Mrs Barker (*calling out*) Gran Twigden, you at 'ome?

Gran (*startled*) Oh! It's you, Ma Barker, you come in.

Mrs Barker (*removing the sacking from her head*) It's rainin' cats an' dogs; peltin' down it is. Oh! I 'ate gettin' my shawl wet, so I puts this ol' sack over me 'ead.

Gran Well, you lay it out over those sticks there, an' dry it out a bit.

Mrs Barker (*joining Gran, she kneels down and spreads out the sack over the sticks*) What lovely sticks you got. Them's sizeable ones, ain't they? You never got those from the Highway.

Gran (*laughing*) No I ain't. I 'ave my own ... secret place. (*She winks*)

Mrs Barker (*still kneeling*) An' where might that be?

Gran Oh! Wouldn't you like to know. It's a heavenly place where you can't move a foot without fallin' over a nice thick stick. It's a sticker's paradise, ain't it!

Mrs Barker (*laughing*) I knows! I knows! Gran Twigden, you've been in his Lordship's park again, 'aven't you?

Gran Maybe I 'ave, an' maybe I 'aven't.

Mrs Barker (*getting up from her kneeling position*) What's wrong with your 'ead? (*She sits*)

Gran I got the toothache bad.

Mrs Barker That red flannel'll not do it much good.

Gran Oh, Sarah swears by it.

Mrs Barker Welsh flannel is good for chesty coughs. Now if you 'ad a chesty cough, an' that red flannel was bound around you, now that *would* work. But I ain't got no confidence in it for toothache.

Gran I'm goin' to give it a try. I says to meself when it's really bad, well ol' girl, it could be worse, it's only teeth, an' it's not goin' to kill you, it's better than a bad pain in the bowels, that's what I think.

Mrs Barker Your toothache reminds me of Gran Perkins, you know, the one who lived opposite the *Red Lion*. When 'er 'usband ran off she 'ad to go into the Workhouse. They took 'er in 'cos she had no ways of keepin' herself. Well, she 'adn't been in there a week before Matron said, "I've 'ad enough of your wailin' and moanin' over those teeth, Mrs Perkins, they are comin' *out*, all of them, and you shall 'ave false ones."

Gran But Gran Perkins 'ad no money for false teeth.

Mrs Barker Of course she didn't. It's only gentry what can afford false teeth. (*She sits down again*) But if you get put in the Workhouse you get them given to you, for nothin', it comes out of the Poor Rate. Last week I was comin' out of the bakers, an' who should be goin' in with 'er daughter but Gran Perkins. She comes out on day release to visit Aggie at the laundry. Well, I could 'ardly believe what I saw. There was Gran Perkins looking twenty years younger, grinnin' at me with two rows of perfect, perfect white teeth! The last time I'd seen 'er she 'ad 'orrible, nasty little black spikes for teeth. But last week 'er teeth, 'er new teeth, took twenty years off 'er looks an' she don't 'ave toothache no more.

Gran Well, it ain't fair! That *she* should 'ave false teeth an' I can't. What you come for anyway?

Mrs Barker Some of your Sarah's liniment for my legs. They've been terrible painful lately.

Sarah opens the door and comes in carrying a bucketful of water. She puts it down, takes off her shawl, gives it a good shake, then drapes it over one of the kitchen chairs

Sarah Oh, hallo Mrs Barker. It's still raining. 'As Mother made you a cup of tea?

Gran We've not 'ad time for tea-drinking.

Sarah (*coming forward*) Well, I should have known you two would be gossipin'! You've not been up for some time, Mrs Barker.

Mrs Barker No. But I've not got any of your liniment left, an' I need it for me varicose veins.

Gran Sarah! Pour Mrs Barker a glass of your parsnip wine, that'll soon make 'er forget 'er varicose veins. (*She chuckles to herself*)

Sarah (*going to the dresser and getting out a bottle and some glasses*) Why don't we all 'ave a glass o' wine?

Mrs Barker Oh! I don't know whether I ought in the middle of the day.

Gran Go on, Ma Barker, it'll put some colour into your cheeks. My Sarah makes the best parsnip wine in the village. The best. I bet 'is Lordship's cellars can't come up with a better tasting wine.

Sarah (*pouring out the wine and handing the glasses to the women*) Oh, Mother, how you exaggerate. It's quite wrong you know, the things you say.

Gran Don't be miserable. Pull 'round that chair, girl, an' join us in our gossip.

Mrs Barker (*drinking great gulps*) My! This is fine wine.

Sarah (*leaning over and then filling Mrs Barker's glass again*) A little of what you fancy does you good. (*She winks*)

Mrs Barker (*giggling*) Oh! I know I shouldn't. But I can't say when I took a glass of wine last.

Gran Talkin' of gossip, is there anythin' we haven't 'eard?

Mrs Barker Well, I don't know what you *'ave* heard, now do I?

Gran No. Just tell us the latest.

Mrs Barker The latest. Well, now let me see. I expect it's about Mrs Thornley of Bishop's Farm. . . .

Gran What about 'er?

Mrs Barker Well, last Friday she went down to 'er youngest girl's cottage along Brookside. 'Er daughter 'ad sent 'er boy runnin' up to the farm in a fright sayin' 'is Father was beatin' 'is Mother in a drunken fit . . . ahm . . . ahm . . . You know this parsnip wine 'as made me throat seem quite dry . . . I can't seem to speak . . .

Gran Sarah! Give 'er a drop more, don't be mean.

Sarah (*pouring out yet another glass for Mrs Barker*) I've never known it make throats *dry*.

Mrs Barker Well, it takes folks differently, don't it? We're not all made the same, are we? (*She takes a sip. During the rest of the scene she becomes noticeably tipsy*) Now, where was I in me tale?

Gran Mrs Thornley went to Brookside.

Mrs Barker Ah! Yes. Well . . . we've all known in the village about 'er son-in-law's drinkin'. He goes 'ome an' beats the livin' daylights out of Lily Thornley, what was . . . (*She sips wine*) Now last Friday Mrs Thornley arrives in the cottage. 'Er Lily is black an' blue with bruises an' sobbin' 'er 'eart out. On the sofa dead drunk is 'er 'usband, fast asleep. 'E's nearly beaten 'er senseless, then fell onto the sofa exhausted . . . (*She sips more wine*)

A Country Rebel

Sarah So what did Mrs Thornley do?

Mrs Barker I'll tell you what she did . . . she said, "Lily! Get me a sheet, a needle an' thread, quick girl!"

Gran An' what did she want with a needle an' thread when 'er daughter was nearly senseless with beatin'?

Mrs Barker If you'll give me a chance, I'll tell you, won't I! (*She pushes her empty glass forward for Sarah to re-fill*) Once the sheet is brought Mrs Thornley rolls 'im off the sofa onto it. She takes off the great belt 'e's wearin', the one 'e beats Lily an' the children with, an' then she gets down on 'er 'ands an' knees an' sews 'im up tightly in the sheet, with only 'is 'ead free. Tight 'e is like a caterpillar in 'is skin.

Sarah Now why should she do a thing like that?

Mrs Barker (*laughing uproariously*) I'll tell you why. So she could give 'im a bit of 'is own medicine. She got that belt of 'is an' she beat 'im until he cried for mercy. But she carried on, she lashed 'im with that great belt of 'is until 'e was stone sober. Then when she'd finished, she knelt down close to 'is ear, an' she said, "Jack Scott, you lay a finger on my Lily an' the children ever again, an' I'll come one night when you're blind drunk, an' next time this sheet will be your shroud, for I'll beat you till you're dead."

Gran That Mrs Thornley always did 'ave some go in 'er. It's all that red 'air of 'ers. Mind, that Lily would 'ave Jack Scott 'as 'er 'usband, though 'e never was good enough.

Mrs Barker Perhaps you're right. My Jack was cow-man to Parson Curry, and your two men were ploughmen to 'is Lordship. Our men were good men, so the Lord took them. (*She begins to cry*) Three poor widows, with not one man between us to give us a slap . . .

Sarah (*taking the glass from her*) Now don't upset yourself.

Gran That wine takes some with a laughin' fit, an' some with a cryin' fit. She done with laughin' an' now 'as to cry. Let 'er be for a minute. She come up for your liniment.

Sarah My leg liniment or my back liniment? (*She gets up, collects the bottle and glasses, puts them on the dresser, stoops down and starts to look in the cupboard*) I know I got plenty of back liniment, there ain't been so many complaints this past winter, but my leg liniment's been popular.

Gran Ay! You're good with legs an' backs. I only wish you 'ad liniment for toothache. (*She grimaces*) It's getting bad again.

Sarah Ah! 'ere it is, my last bottle. She won't go away disappointed. (*She comes forward*) You're in luck, Mrs Barker, I got one left.

Mrs Barker (*rousing herself*) Oh, good! My poor ol' legs been aching with the strain on 'em. Something awful it's been. Now tuppence, ain't it?

Sarah That's right. Tuppence a bottle.

Mrs Barker (*taking the money out of a purse she keeps in her skirt pocket*) Tuppence well spent I says. Give it me, I'll put it 'ere in my apron pocket where it'll be safe, there ... (*She pats the pocket*) I can't wait to get 'ome an' put it on. (*She stands up, but has to steady herself*) Oops ... I feels ... I feels ... (*She straightens herself*) I feels a lot better than when I come up, I can tell you. (*She bends down and picks up her sack*) Oh! This is quite dry.

Sarah I don't think you'll need it. (*She goes to door and opens it. A ray of sunshine illuminates her*) Look, the sun's out. It's going to be a fine day after all. You'll enjoy your walk back to the village.

Mrs Barker exits

For a moment Sarah stands in the doorway, then shades her eyes against the sun, and peers down the lane

Sarah I think that's the postman comin' up our lane, Mother.

Gran (*turning around*) What's 'e doin' comin' up our lane then? We be the only people up this way.

Sarah I do believe 'e's wavin' a letter at me. 'E's got somethin' in 'is 'and. (*She peers even harder*) It is a letter, Mother, an' 'e's grinnin' an' shoutin' somethin'. Oh! I've got to go down an' meet 'im.

Sarah rushes out, leaving the door ajar. The sunlight floods into the cottage. The sound of birds can be heard

Gran sits strumming the arms of her chair impatiently

Gran Oh! I can't sit 'ere no longer, what's Sarah up to? (*She gets up and turns towards the door*)

Sarah enters in an excited mood

Sarah You'll never guess, Mother, it's a letter from our Edgar. (*She waves a letter in the air*) It's got an American post-mark, look! (*She moves forward to show her mother*)

A Country Rebel

Gran (*taking the letter*) Well I never, a letter from our Edgar, all the way from America (*She stands there looking at it*)

Sarah Oh! Come on, Mother, open it, see what it says.

Gran (*beginning to cry*) Oh! I can't, Sarah. It's brought it all back to me. Edgar was such a lovely little boy, always kissin' an' huggin' me. I know it, Sarah, I loved 'im then more than you girls. (*She wipes her eyes with her apron*) It were too much love I gave 'im an' God punished me for it by takin' 'im away.

Sarah (*going up to her*) There's no need to carry on like that.

Gran (*sitting down*) No, it weren't right my favourin' 'im the way I did.

Sarah Well! Aren't you goin' to open the letter an' see what 'e says?

Gran No! I've cried till me eyes are all red. You read it to me, Sarah.

Sarah (*taking the letter and sitting down opposite her mother*) Now let's see then. (*She is just about to tear it open with her finger nail, when her mother stops her*)

Gran Nay, Sarah! Don't tear it open all awkward like. You go fetch a knife an' slice it open dainty like.

Sarah (*going to dresser*) Now if it were a letter from me, or Liza, you'd not be so fussy.

Gran A letter that's come all that way is somethin' special. T'aint everyone in the village what gets mail from America.

Sarah (*opening letter*) From the *United* States of America, Mother. Get it right. (*She comes forward again*)

Gran Come on girl, read it an' lets know what 'e 'as to say.

Sarah (*reading slowly from the letter, not having been a good scholar at school*) "Dear Mother, we are still all fine. The boys are to be apprenticed tool-makers, which pleases me enormously. It sure is swell to know that they will be settled in a trade. Even out here in Pennsylvania a man needs a good trade if he is to get on in life. This year the winter was a bad one with twenty-four inches of snow, and bitter freezing winds most days. But this letter ain't about the weather it's to tell you that we are coming over to see you. . . ." (*She breaks off in amazement*)

Gran (*astounded*) What! Comin' over to see me. So 'e's took it into 'is 'ead to come an' see me. Does the letter say anythin' else?

Sarah Ay, it goes on a bit. (*She continues to read*) "I'm bringin' Janey over too. As you've never met my dear wife, it seems only proper to bring 'er over. That way she can get to know 'er folks back home. She will find it strange being in a village, as she is used to Philadelphia: You will make her welcome I know. We shall be there for the harvest as I want Janey to see how things are done at harvest time. It is a time when many of the old boys come back, and we can enjoy the jollifications that take place then. This will give you some months to prepare for us. Please give our love to Sarah and the others. And there is a big hug and kiss for you. Edgar."

Gran Such a fine letter. 'E always was a scholar.

Sarah This cottage will need some tidyin' up, won't it?

Gran We must give the walls a coat of whitewash.

Sarah (*putting the letter back into the envelope and giving it to her*) There, Mother, you put it in the chest. (*She stands up*) It's time for me to start gettin' our dinner all ready. You sit there now while I get things ready. (*She busies herself at the table, setting it out with cutlery, and other such things*)

Gran Humph! Why my Edgar 'ad to emigrate I don't know. 'E was 'appy up the manor in 'is Lordship's stables.

Sarah (*interrupting*) Edgar always 'ad ambition. 'E went away because 'e knew 'e could do better than work in 'is Lordship's stables, an' look what 'e's done. 'E's a foreman, in a steelworks.

Gran (*mollified*) Well, I suppose you's right. I'd best be lookin' forward to seein' 'im. But ... Oh! Sarah, it be twenty years, what is 'e goin' to think of 'is poor ol' mother all bound up with red Welsh flannel. What a sight I shall make!

Sarah (*coming to centre stage*) Don't fret, 'e'll love you, Mother, like 'e always did.

Gran (*starting to cry again*) I've grown old an' worn out, I 'ave. 'E'll remember me as I was. What a sight I shall be ... If only I could be like Gran Perkins an' 'ave false teeth an' look twenty years younger. I'd wish that, Sarah! To 'ave false teeth.

Sarah Oh! Mother, we ain't got no money. It's only gentry what buys false teeth.

Gran Gran Perkins 'as false teeth, an' she ain't gentry!

Sarah I knows that! But she be in the Workhouse. The Parish paid for 'er teeth.

Gran (*in a determined manner*) Then that's what I got to do, go into the Workhouse!

Sarah (*alarmed*) Now, Mother! What can you mean? There's no need for you to go into the Workhouse. My doin' laundry for Mrs Dodds keeps us together.

Gran But Sarah, don't you see! If I goes into the Workhouse, I'll get me false teeth. Matron will see me awful pegs an' order them out. I need only stay until I gets me false teeth, then out I come. You can ask for my release.

Sarah (*sitting down beside the fire*) The Guardians would never admit you. They knows you live with me 'ere in the cottage.

Gran Oh, Sarah, use your 'ead! I'm an ol' girl, ain't I? An' there's many like me what goes crazy, an' can't be left for fear they falls in the fire. You got to write a note to the Guardians sayin' you want me admitted 'cos I 'ave crazy fits.

Sarah Oh! I don't know. Will it work. . . . What will the village say?

Gran A pot on the village, that's what I say! If I can see my Edgar with new teeth an' lookin' twenty years younger, then I couldn't care a cuss what the village says.

Sarah But *I* care. I don't like 'em gossipin' about me.

Gran Sticks an' stones may break my bones, but words they cannot hurt me.

Sarah (*exasperated*) Oh! You've always got a smart answer for everything.

Gran That's 'cos I'm smart, see.

Sarah (*pleading*) But I don't want you to go.

Gran It's only 'til I get me teeth.

Sarah Why are you so stubborn about it?

Gran 'Cos my Edgar's bringin' his wife 'ere, an' I want good lookin' teeth for that American to see. It's a matter o' pride.

Sarah It's a matter o' vanity!

Gran Well! Are you goin' to be a good girl an' help me? Or not?

Sarah Oh! All right, Mother. (*She gets up*) I'll do it now before dinner. I'll say you're goin' crazy, an' I want you admitted to the Workhouse 'cos I can't look after you no more. (*She begins to get out paper, envelopes and pen; as she does so the lights begin to fade*)

Gran That's it. An' when I've 'ad all me teeth out, I'll come back 'ome looking twenty years younger. Like when our Edgar left. Like when 'e first went away.

The lights are dimmed to denote the passing of time; when they come up again a week later, we see Sarah standing at the kitchen table sorting out a pile of laundry; beside her Gran is diligently mending a shirt

Hilda, the young daughter of Sarah, now a housemaid at the manor, comes into the cottage in a state of some agitation

Hilda (*closing the door*) Oh! I'm glad to have caught you both together. It will save me time, for her Ladyship said I'm not to stop, but just prepare you for her visit.

Sarah A visit! From her Ladyship. Glory be, what 'ave we done, child? (*She sits heavily in the chair*) Oh! Hilda, what 'ave we done?

Hilda From what I can make out she's been told that you're putting Gran in the Workhouse, and she won't have it!

Gran Ugh! I could cuss, I could use some fine language!

Hilda But Gran, I can't believe you'd want to go into the Workhouse. It's a terrible place.

Gran Don't you fret. I reckon I'll meet some of my ol' pals in there.

Hilda Mother! How can you make arrangements for Gran to be admitted, knowing what sort of place it is?

Sarah (*perturbed*) Hilda, I don't want.... It ain't me what's...

Gran (*interrupting*) Sarah! Say no more. This 'ere problem is between your mother an' me, see Hilda. (*She takes her granddaughter's hand*) Now I knows you love your ol' granny, an' wants 'er 'appy 'ere, but I've decided to give your Ma a rest see!

Hilda You won't rest in the Workhouse. I been told there's terrible shriekings and goings on at night.

Gran P'raps people add a bit o' colour to their stories.

Hilda (*not convinced*) Oh! I do hope her Ladyship can change your mind. She said she was shocked to hear that my mother would put her own flesh and blood in the Workhouse.

Gran (*sniffing with disapproval*) There's many a poor woman that's 'ad no choice in the matter. T'aint nothin' to do with flesh an' blood; 'tis to do with bein' poor, an' the gentry never givin' us enough to save on. An' Hilda, if I wants to go into the Workhouse, then 'er Ladyship ain't goin' to stop me.

Hilda I'm sure she can if she wishes. Her Ladyship always has her own way.

Gran (*sitting before the fire with a determined look on her face*) Oh, does she now. Well, she may be able to twist 'is Lordship 'round 'er little finger, but when I makes up my mind to do a thing, then I does it. I be a destitute widow, livin' 'ere through the kindness of my daughter. I can claim to be a pauper and no-one can say I ain't!

Hilda (*sitting at the table in tears*) Oh! The shame of it. How can I ever hold my head up proud again, with my Gran in the Workhouse? I'll die of shame.

Sarah (*looking perturbed and going over to Hilda*) Now, now, Hilda, don't cry like that, t'isn't worth it. (*She turns with a pleading look at Gran*) P'raps Gran will change 'er mind. Gran, say you'll think on it, say you'll think again. It's not what *I* want, an' you can see 'ow upset our Hilda is. T'aint fair!

Gran There's many a thing in life t'aint fair!

Hilda (*looking up*) Well I want you to know that I'll die of shame!

Gran (*sniffing*) As far as I knows, shame never killed anyone, an' I knows a lot o' people what ought to 'ave died of shame.

Hilda Oh, Gran. No-one can ever shift you when you've made up your mind. (*She stands, drying her eyes with a handkerchief*) I'd better be off. Her Ladyship is coming down the Mulberry Walk to see you. She'll be here any minute. (*She makes one final plea to Gran*) Please Gran, think again about going into the Workhouse.

Gran All right, all right, just don't badger me now. 'Er Ladyship will be badgerin' me enough as it is. Comin' down 'ere stickin' 'er nose in!

Hilda leaves, her mother following her to the door and kissing her goodbye. The cottage door is left slightly ajar to allow sunshine to flood in

Sarah Now, Gran, you must behave yourself. I'll not 'ave you upset 'er Ladyship.

Gran It's 'er! *She* be the one what gets all 'eated up. I'm goin' to get my false teeth by 'ook or by crook, an' she ain't goin' to stop me.

Sarah (*dismayed*) Oh! I knows it, I can see it. You're goin' to get all nasty with 'er, an' this is a tied cottage. 'Is Lordship by the kindness of 'is 'eart lets us 'ave this cottage free as widows of 'is ploughmen. Oh! God, you'll 'ave me thrown out, evicted.

Gran I'll only be sharp with 'er, if she's sharp with *me*.

Sarah You'll not be sharp at all! You watch your manners with your betters, Gran.

Gran I'm promisin' nothin'.

Sarah (*gleefully*) I've got it! You pretend you're fast asleep 'ere in front of the fire. (*She kneels down and simulates poking the fire*)

Gran Sleepin', I never sleep in the middle of the day, never!

Sarah (*standing up*) Now look 'ere, Mother. You'd better pretend to be sleepin' or I'll change my mind an' say I wouldn't dream of puttin' you in the Workhouse. I'll say I've changed my mind, an' there'll be no fine new false teeth for you to greet Edgar with.

Gran (*bad tempered*) All right! All right! Spoil my little bit o' fun with 'er Ladyship. 'Tis a rotten world when an ol' girl like me can't tell 'er betters what she thinks of 'em.

Sarah Now get yourself settled, come on, close those eyes, an' look as if you be in a deep sleep. 'Er Ladyship will be 'ere soon. Come on, you always says you're good at actressing, now you actress an' pretend you're asleep.

Sarah goes back to the table, sits and folds linen neatly into piles

There is a shadow in the doorway, and Lady Corbishley enters. She is a well-preserved woman of around fifty

Sarah springs up immediately and curtsies

Lady Corbishley Ah! Mrs Dawkins, I am so pleased to find you at home. I sent Hilda down to make sure you were here. One does not want to waste one's valuable time in coming down to an empty cottage, does one?

Sarah (*curtsying again*) No, your Ladyship.

Lady Corbishley (*coming into the centre of the room*) These cottages are quite cramped, are they not? One cannot imagine from the outside how terribly cramped they are on the inside. (*She stands beside a chair*)

Sarah rushes round the table, pulls out the chair and carefully places it behind her Ladyship in order for her to sit down

Thank you, Mrs Dawkins. Yes.... (*She looks around*) Quite, quite cramped.

Sarah (*stepping back into the centre of the room*) It's big enough for our needs, your Ladyship.

Lady Corbishley Oh! Naturally, it is probably just the right size

now, but how on earth did you manage when you had all those girls living at home? How many was it? Five?
Sarah Ay! Your Ladyship, five little girls.
Lady Corbishley And two bedrooms I believe?
Sarah Ay! Your Ladyship. But when I 'ad Hilda I put 'er in a drawer out of the dresser.
Lady Corbishley How cosy! What a cosy way of solving the problem. Quite ingenuous.
Sarah I 'opes our Hilda pleases your Ladyship?
Lady Corbishley Ah! Yes, always willing to learn, that girl. But I've not come here to talk about Hilda.
Sarah No, your Ladyship.
Lady Corbishley It's Mrs Twigden there, indeed, I was hoping to have a word with her. She seems to be sleeping.
Sarah (*glancing nervously at Gran, who snores*) Yes! Your Ladyship, she be sound asleep. I gave 'er a drop o' Godfrey's Cordial which I 'ad left over from the girls.
Lady Corbishley Godfrey's Cordial! But that's full of opium.
Sarah Oh! I don't know what it's full of, your Ladyship, but it always did the trick with my girls when they was ill, sent them to sleep in no time at all.
Lady Corbishley (*annoyed*) And I *did* want a word with her. Do you realize that she has been lying. . . . I mean telling fibs . . . to Lady Isabella and Lady Jane? Lady Isabella was in the High Street when she met your mother, who told her it was her birthday, and what a lucky omen Lady Isabella was, for her anniversary. Naturally, Lady Isabella gave her a sovereign and wished her well. Three weeks later she told the same story to Lady Jane who was coming out of the Rectory. Two sovereigns in three weeks! Two birthdays in the same year, Mrs Dawkins. Most odd!
Sarah Oh! I'm sure my mother meant no 'arm.
Lady Corbishley Yes! Well that brings me to the real purpose of my visit. The Guardians at the Workhouse have notified me that your mother has applied for admission. His Lordship and I have decided that as the widow of one of our estate workers we cannot permit this.

Gran snores loudly, startling her Ladyship

We have decided to give her a small pension of three shillings a week. In this way she will not be destitute, and have no need to apply for admission. As you know the fall in grain prices has reduced our income considerably. We cannot possibly afford to give all the estate widows pensions, but in your mother's case, we make an exception.

Gran snores even louder

Does Godfrey's Cordial usually induce such chronic snoring?

Sarah It was an old bottle, your Ladyship, p'raps it makes a difference.

Lady Corbishley It is most disturbing. (*She rises*) So the matter is settled, three shillings a week and she remains here with you.

Gran snores loudly

Sarah (*glancing over at Gran*) But your Ladyship ... I knows you an' 'is Lordship is most kind ... but ... but ...

Lady Corbishley But what!

Sarah Well, I be sendin' 'er into the Workhouse 'cos she's crazy these days, she be out of 'er mind most days ... I can't leave 'er for fear she falls in the fire. She loses 'er balance and falls down, or she plays with the fire in a crazy fashion. She's got to go into the Workhouse for 'er own safety, your Ladyship.

Gran gives a great snore then slumps forward in her chair, and gives the impression she might fall into the fire

Oh! God, there she goes! Oh! Beggin' your Ladyship's pardon.

Sarah goes over and gently pushes her mother back upright in the chair

Lady Corbishley Oh! Very well. One cannot fight senility. But I may warn you that one of the lady Guardians, Mrs Miles-Foster, will be calling today to interview your mother. I'd see that she comes out of that deep sleep if I were you. (*She turns to go, but pauses*) And don't give her any more of that Godfrey's Cordial. If it's as old as you say, it could be highly dangerous.

Sarah Well, I reckon she won't be with us much longer, she be very frail.

Lady Corbishley It's very odd, but when I caught her sticking a week or so ago she seemed perfectly sane to me, and certainly not frail. But then, she always was an odd woman. (*She goes to the door*)

Sarah (*going after her to open the door wide*) Does it mean then, your Ladyship, that if she goes into the Workhouse she won't get that small pension you spoke of?

Lady Corbishley (*pausing*) She won't need it in the Infirmary. It was intended to keep her here with you.

Sarah Now that be a great shame. For she do like 'er little comforts.

Lady Corbishley (*reflecting upon all this*) Oh, very well. We shall arrange to have her three shillings a week remitted to the Master at the Workhouse. He can see to the buying of any "comforts". Good-day, Mrs Dawkins.

Sarah (*curtsying*) Good-day, your Ladyship, thankin' your Ladyship for comin'. Gran will be grateful for the pension.

Lady Corbishley exits. Sarah closes the door firmly behind her. Then leans against it laughing

Oh God! I shall die laughin', them's goin' to give me Mother a pension!

Gran (*now alert and also highly amused*) Sarah! You be good at actressing too! (*She stands up*) An' I got meself a pension.

Sarah You can buy yourself dozens of marzipan cakes.

Gran Ay! An' when I got my false teeth they won't give me toothache after, now will they?

Sarah Now you're goin' to 'ave to speak with this Mrs Miles-Foster, Gran, so you make sure you says the right things.

Gran Oh! Sarah, you got it right when you said I be mad, why that's the answer to all this. I'll be a crazy ol' woman. (*Laughing*) I'll frighten the livin' daylights out of 'er, won't I?

Sarah Mother! Now don't go too wild. You know 'ow you gets when you're all excited.

Gran (*going back to fireside*) All right, girl, don't go on at me. I knows where to draw the line.

Sarah Well I 'opes so.

There is a knock at the cottage door. Sarah goes to answer it

Mrs Miles-Foster enters. A smartly dressed woman of indeterminate age

Mrs Miles-Foster (*peeling off gloves*) I'm so glad you are at home, Mrs Dawkins. I have just met Lady Corbishley. She tells me that admission to the Workhouse is sought because of your mother's senility. Is that so?

Sarah Won't you sit down, ma'am, an' we can talk about it. (*She motions to a kitchen chair*)

Mrs Miles-Foster Thank you, but I prefer to sit near your mother. I need to ascertain her state of mind in order to give her an admission slip for the Master. I see she is sleeping beside the fire. (*She crosses to the hearth*)

Sarah (*going forward, and shaking her mother*) Mother dear, one of the Guardians is 'ere to ask you some questions.

Gran (*waking up with a start*) Don't you call me Mother! I ain't your Ma.

Sarah Will you answer the lady's questions when she puts them to you?

Gran Questions? Oh! I like questions—they ask me questions at school. I sits in the front desk an' when the mistress asks me a question I allus knows the answer. I allus do!

Mrs Miles-Foster (*sitting down*) Perhaps you could leave this to me, Mrs Dawkins.

Sarah turns and sits at the kitchen table

Now, Mrs Twigden, I believe your daughter has requested that you be admitted to the Workhouse as a pauper.

Gran Pauper! I be no pauper. My father be a rich gentleman, 'e be. Draw your chair a mite closer, see, 'cos that there woman there, she be my foster mother.

Mrs Miles-Foster moves her chair nearer Gran's

Mrs Miles-Foster Mrs Twigden, that poor woman is your daughter Sarah.

Gran She's not me daughter, she's me foster mother, what's lookin' after me.

Mrs Miles-Foster I think you are confused, Mrs Twigden. You are getting things muddled up. Now Lady Corbishley is to arrange for you to have a pension of three shillings a week. That will enable you to stay here with your daughter.

Gran (*putting out her arm, and clutching Mrs Miles-Foster*) Oh! Do you see them? Those nasty, evil goblins in the fire! (*She

A Country Rebel

points hysterically) They come see, down the chimney an' 'ide in the coals, then when they be ready they casts spells on us, evil nasty spells. (*She stands up and takes off her shawl*) Oh! They be nasty little red devils. Yes! That's what they be, nasty red devils with red 'ot pins, an' they're pointin' them at you! (*She flings her shawl over Mrs Miles-Foster, crushing her hat*)

Mrs Miles-Foster struggles to get the shawl off her head and shoulders

Mrs Miles-Foster Good gracious, woman, there is no need for this! (*Freeing herself*) That is a perfectly harmless fire. You have completely dishevelled me. My hat must be quite crushed!

Gran Oh! Lord. Oh! Lord, there's a big blackbird what's come on your shoulder. It's goin' to peck off your nose. (*She goes into the middle of the room and dances around*) "The maid was in the garden 'anging out the clothes and down came a blackbird an' pecked off 'er nose."

Mrs Miles-Foster (*getting up*) Mrs Dawkins, it is quite obvious that your poor mother is mad, quite mad. I shall give you an admission note and you can take her in this afternoon. (*She sits at the kitchen table*) Just bring her along as she is. (*She writes*) Good, clean, wholesome clothes will be issued to her upon arrival. There is no need for you to bring any of her things. Personal possessions are not encouraged. (*She finishes the note*) Here, show this upon arrival. (*She stands up, tries to straighten her hat again*) Please endeavour to quieten her down before you walk over: we don't like to admit them in a state of frenzy, it frightens the others in the Infirmary.

Sarah (*going to the door*) Oh! You've taken a load off my mind, I can tell you. I can sleep in peace now, ma'am.

Mrs Miles-Foster (*going out*) I'm sure that you can. Good-day, Mrs Dawkins.

Sarah (*curtsying*) Good-day, ma'am.

Mrs Miles-Foster exits

Sarah again closes the door firmly. Both women go to the door, listen for her steps, then after a second or two burst into laughter

Gran Oh! We done it! We 'ave bamboozled them good an' proper. Oh! I've never done such fine actressing. I *did* enjoy it so.

Sarah Come on, Mother, let's put our shawls on and get goin'. It'll take us some time to walk casual like over to the Workhouse. An' I can't wait to get on with the drama.

They both laugh uproariously

Gran (*fastening shawl*) I knows what we'll do, Sarah. We'll go into *Red Lion* on way an' get us a dinner o' beef an' pickles, an' a couple o' gins. We deserve it, don't us?

Sarah (*folding shawl over her head*) I ain't got no money for beef an' pickles.

Gran (*laughing*) But I 'ave, ain't I? I be rich, I got meself a couple of sovereigns, ain't I?

Sarah You wicked ol' girl, takin' in poor Lady Isabella, an' poor Lady Jane with talk o' your birthday. Why you ain't got a birthday 'til next December seventh.

Gran I knows when me birthday is. But I got the money, didn't I?

Sarah Yes! An' where you keepin' it?

Gran In me boot. (*She holds up a leg*) That's the safest place for money. That's where I used to put the odd copper I made as a girl. Me mother would find it if I put it anywhere else, but in me boot it was allus safe.

Sarah Come on then, Ma, it's beef an' pickles for us, to celebrate.

Gran An' a couple o' gins! Don't forget the gin! An' in a month I'll have me new teeth, an' you can 'ave me released! 'Ome I'll come with teeth ...

Sarah I should be worried about you if you was not such a tough ol' girl. (*She tidies up the fireplace*)

Gran No, don't worry 'bout me. Matron ain't goin' to fright me with 'er bossiness.

Sarah An' you save a bit o' that three shillin' pension you be gettin'.

Gran (*laughing*) An' I intends to live 'til I'm ninety-nine. Oh! 'Er Ladyship will be in a frenzy when she counts up all those shillin's I'll be gettin'.

Sarah An' think of all those marzipan cakes you can guzzle ...

Gran (*at the door*) Without getting a bit o' toothache.

Sarah Oh, Ma, a life without toothache. What a wonderful thought. Why, *I* might want false teeth meself ...

Gran My turn first, Sarah! It was *my* idea. So it's my turn first. You can 'ave your teeth next year when you 'ave *your* crazy turn. 'Cos madness runs in families. We all knows that! Next year it's your turn, Sarah.

They both laugh uproariously

Let's get a move on.

The women exit

Blackout

CURTAIN

FURNITURE AND PROPERTY LIST

On stage: Fender to denote hearth of fireplace
Chairs
Wooden table. *On it:* saucepan, bowl, *in it:* potatoes, knife
Pail of water
Ramshackle dresser. *In it:* bottle of oil of clove, roll of red flannel, bottle of parsnip wine, glasses, bottle of liniment, knife, paper, envelopes and pen, cutlery. *On it:* oddments of china, bowl. *In it:* safety pin, needle and cotton
Hook in the wall
Pile of laundry

Off stage: Great bundle of twigs (**Gran**)
Letter (**Sarah**)
Note, pen (**Mrs Miles-Foster**)

Personal: **Gran**: rag
Hilda: handkerchief
Mrs Barker: purse, *in it:* loose change

LIGHTING PLOT

Property fittings required: *nil*

Interior. The same scene throughout

To open: Interior lighting. Dull exterior lighting

Cue 1	**Sarah:** "Tuppence a bottle." *Brighten exterior lighting*	(Page 8)
Cue 2	**Sarah** begins to get out paper, envelopes and pen *Lights begin to dim*	(Page 11)
Cue 3	**Gran:** "... when 'e first went away." *Lights dim to denote the passage of a week; then are brought up again when ready*	(Page 11)

EFFECTS PLOT

Cue 1 **Sarah** rushes out leaving the door ajar (Page 8)
Sound of birds

www.ingramcontent.com/pod-product-compliance
Lightning Source LLC
Chambersburg PA
CBHW070455050426
42450CB00012B/3291